19.00

tary

$)$

★ SPORTS STARS ★

SHAQUILLE O'NEAL
BIG MAN, BIG DREAMS

BY MARK STEWART

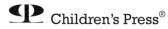

Children's Press®
A Division of Grolier Publishing
New York London Hong Kong Sydney
Danbury, Connecticut

Photo Credits
Photographs ©: Allsport USA: 18, 44 (Bob Daemrich), 19 (Jim Gund), 3, 45, 38, 39 (Jed Jacobsohn), 29 (Andy Lyons), 21 (Brian Spurlock); Louisiana State University: 13; NBA Photos: 24, 44, 9, 10, 40, 41, 43, 46 (Andrew D. Bernstein), 11, 27, 33, 36 (Nathaniel Butler), 26 (Brian Drake), 6 (Andy Hayt), 17 (Andy King); SportsChrome East/West: 22, 30 (Brian Drake), 33, 35, 45 (Rich Kane), cover, 14, 47, (Michael Zito); Vandystadt: 37 (Laurent Zabulon).

Visit Children's Press on the Internet at:
http://publishing.grolier.com

Library of Congress Cataloging-in-Publication Data

Stewart, Mark.
   Shaquille O'Neal : big man, big dreams / by Mark Stewart.
     p. cm. — (Sports stars)
     Summary: A biography of the Los Angeles Lakers' high-scoring center, who also owns restaurants and a clothing line, has written books, recorded rap albums, and starred in three films.
     ISBN: 0-516-20970-1 (lib. bdg.)   0-516-26423-0 (pbk.)
     1. O'Neal, Shaquille—Juvenile literature. 2. Basketball players—United States—Biography—Juvenile literature. [1. O'Neal, Shaquille.
     2. Basketball players. 3. Afro-Americans—Biography.] I. Title. II. Series.
GV884.054S85   1998
796.323'092—dc21
[B]   97-32105
                             CIP
                             AC

∗ CONTENTS ∗

★ 1 ★

SHOWTIME!

Wham! Shaquille O'Neal blocks an opponent's shot, slamming it against the glass and sending it bouncing back toward the foul line. A Laker guard retrieves the loose ball and quickly moves downcourt. He pulls up at the top of the key, fakes a pass to his right and dishes off to his left. As the defense rotates to shut down the lane, the ball is lofted softly over the stunned defenders toward the basket. They know what is about to happen, and all they can do is get out of the way. Shaq comes out of nowhere, flying through the air. With his two enormous hands, he grasps the ball above the basket, hammers it down in one smooth motion, then hangs on the rim for a second to savor his monster jam. The crowd leaps to its feet. "Showtime" has returned to Los Angeles's Great Western Forum.

★ 2 ★

ALWAYS ON THE MOVE

Few names roll off the tongue like Shaquille O'Neal. That is what his mother, Lucille, liked so much about it. She lived in a housing project in Newark, New Jersey, and many of her friends and neighbors were members of a religious movement called the Nation of Islam. Although Lucille was not a follower of the Muslim faith, she thought Islamic names sounded interesting and special, so she decided on Shaquille Rashaun for her first-born son. That means Little Warrior. Shaq did not stay little for long.

Shaq's father left Lucille before he was born. While she was pregnant she met a man named Phil Harrison; they fell in love and were married two years later. Both Lucille and Phil worked for

Shaq and his mother, Lucille

the City of Newark. Their jobs did not pay very well, and they lived in a dangerous neighborhood. Phil decided that his family deserved a better life, so he enlisted in the army. Phil was very good at his job. In fact, he was so good that the army began transferring him to a new base every few years.

Moving often was difficult for Shaq. He was much taller than the other boys in his class, and they made fun of him. They thought he was older than they were, and they assumed that he had learning problems and had been held back several grades. They also teased him about his name. Shaq usually responded by beating up his new schoolmates, which did not help. "It took a while to gain friends," he admits. "Kids just naturally thought I was mean, which was a logical

Today, Shaq is warm and friendly, but he often got into fights when he was younger.

conclusion because I was big, always fighting." By the time classmates realized what a smart, funny, and nice guy he was, it was time to move again. He had to start all over with a new group of kids.

Shaq showed off all the time. He talked constantly in class and tried to distract other kids, which often earned him a trip to the principal's office. He also wrote graffiti, set off fire alarms, and took things that did not belong to him. Because everyone knows everyone else around an army base, Shaq would almost always be caught and punished. Shaq does not know for sure why he was so difficult, but he has an idea. "There was always a lot of love in our house," he says. "But it didn't seem enough for me. I was always trying to get attention and so I acted like a juvenile delinquent."

Shaq was 10 years old when his family made the biggest move of all. Phil was transferred to a base in Wildflecken, Germany. He and Lucille took Shaq and their other children, Ayesha, Lateefah, and Jamal, to a place where English was a foreign language and where there were almost no black faces to be found once they left the base.

Shaq felt even more out of place, and his behavior was worse than ever. His mother and father had a big problem on their hands, and they knew it was only going to get bigger. They decided that they would punish him severely when he did bad but praise him highly when he did good. It took a while for this strategy to work, but it eventually did. Shaq stopped being a troublemaker. By the time he was a teenager, he had his sights set on a career in basketball.

Shaq's father, Phil Harrison

✮ 3 ✮

A STAR IS BORN

Shaquille O'Neal had been playing hoops since he was eight years old. He learned the fundamentals of the game from Phil, who was a big fan of the Boston Celtics. For 25 years, the team had run an offense based on a mobile, multitalented center, and this was the way Phil wanted his boy to play. Shaq learned to move to the ball, operate away from the basket, and make things happen for himself and his teammates. "He's a strong man," says Shaq of Phil, the man he calls his father, "and he always tried to transfer that strength to me on the basketball court. 'Your ball, your court, your game,' that's what he used to tell me."

LSU coach Dale Brown realized that Shaq had the potential to become a star.

One day, Dale Brown, the basketball coach for Louisiana State University, stopped by the base in Germany to give the enlisted men a basketball clinic. Phil suggested that Shaq stop by the gym and listen to Brown. After all, it was never too early to start thinking about a possible college scholarship. After the clinic ended, Shaq asked Coach Brown to suggest a weight training program to help him build up his knees, ankles, and thighs. Brown asked Shaq how long he had been in the army. When Shaq told him he was only 13, Brown got very excited. He asked to meet with Shaq's father, and a few minutes later the LSU coach was giving Sergeant Harrison his big recruiting speech.

Shaq is one of the few NBA centers who failed to make his high school team as a freshman.

---- ★ ★ ★ ----

Phil told him that he wanted to know what LSU could do for his boy after basketball. There were no guarantees in sports, and Phil wanted to make sure that Shaq got an education. When Brown returned to the United States, there was a letter from Germany on his desk. Shaq had written him that he was interested in playing for him some day.

Shaq did not make his high school team as a ninth grader. His legs were wobbly, and his inside game suffered from his poor jumping ability. Many tall boys go through this stage, and many give up on basketball at the very time they should be trying hardest to improve. Shaq was not about to quit. "I just kept practicing every day," he remembers. "When everybody was going to parties, I was outside dribbling, working on my coordination, and trying to dunk."

———————— ★ ★ ★ ————————

Within a year, Shaq had begun to put it all together. He was 6'7" tall, highly coordinated, and his basketball fundamentals were strong. Because he was growing so fast, he suffered from Osgood-Schlatter disease, which causes excruciating pain in the knees. For years, Shaq had to take massive amounts of calcium, but by the time he was a 10th grader the worst of it was behind him. He made the team and dominated his opponents all season long. At the end of the year, Phil was transferred to a base in San Antonio, Texas. Shaq was sad to leave his friends and teammates behind, but the timing could not have been better for his basketball career.

When the fall semester began at San Antonio's Cole High School in 1987, basketball coach Dave Madura had no idea what was about to happen to his team. His eyes practically popped out of his head when Shaq ducked into his office to say hello. He had grown to 6'9" and his body

Shaq gives a glimpse of things to come with a monster dunk for the Cole High Cougars.

Shaq proudly wears a medal after winning the state championship.

had filled out to 235 pounds. Needless to say, Coach Madura was ecstatic about his new center. The Cole High Cougars won 32 games in a row before losing in the semifinals of the state tournament. In his senior year, Shaq continued to improve. He averaged more than 32 points, 22 rebounds, and 8 blocks a game, and he was honored as a high school All-American. The Cougars went 36–0 and won the state championship against Liberty Hill, the team that had eliminated them from the tournament the year before. Shaq burned them for 40 points in the final and shut down his opponents on defense. On one play he stole a pass, dribbled the length of the floor, and nearly destroyed the backboard with a monster dunk.

Shaq was the most heavily recruited basketball player in America. But his parents were just as proud of the fact that he graduated with a solid B average. In just a few years he had gone from being a feared, misunderstood bully to a student-body leader and one of the most popular kids in his school. When it came time to select a college, Shaq thought about a number of schools. But the first experience with Coach Brown kept coming back to him. In the end, he selected LSU, in Baton Rouge, Louisiana.

Shaq has never regretted joining Coach Brown's basketball program at LSU.

⭐ 4 ⭐

HE'S GRRRREAT!

After a brief period of homesickness, Shaquille O'Neal settled into college life and started having a great time. He seemed to get along with everyone, and he lived life as much like a normal student as a 7'1" celebrity could. When he was not in class or in the gym, Shaq studied in his dormitory, worked on his rap music, and played video games.

When the LSU Tigers opened their season, Shaq was their center. Stanley Roberts, the center on the previous year's team, moved to power forward. And Chris Jackson, a high-scoring second-year guard, was the key man in the backcourt. Each player ranked among

Shaq has been a dominant defensive player since his
freshman year at LSU.

the best in the country at his position, and many experts thought the Tigers could win the national championship. Unfortunately, it did not work out that way. Shaq was not used to playing defense against so many big, fast opponents. He spent a lot of time on the bench because he got into foul trouble. With Shaq off the floor, the Tigers struggled. Still, they finished with a very good 23–9 record, and Shaq established a new conference record for blocked shots.

During his second year in Baton Rouge, Shaq began to develop the offensive moves he needed thanks to a little one-on-one tutoring from Kareem Abdul-Jabbar,

Basketball legend Kareem Abdul-Jabbar, from whom Shaq received valuable tutoring

the highest scoring center of all time. Shaq also worked with Hall of Famer Bill Walton on his two specialties: passing out of the double-team and preventing an opponent from getting the ball close to the basket. A quick learner, Shaq was a first-team All-American and College Player of the Year by season's end. He also was voted the top amateur athlete in the world, an honor that came with a $5,000 prize. Shaq donated the money to a children's charity in Newark.

Although Shaq was honored as an All-American again in 1990–91, his junior season was no fun at all. Because of all the awards he had won, Shaq became a target for opponents. When the referees were not looking, they poked him with their elbows and knees. When the ball was loose, other players always seemed to smash into him. He might have been 7'1" and weighed 300 pounds, but he was still a pussycat at heart. And everyone knew it.

Shaq jams the ball during his fabulous junior year.

A call from his grandmother in New Jersey changed all that. She did not know much about basketball, but she had been watching him on television and told him that he needed to stop smiling and get tough. From that point on he had a monster season. But his teammates were not good enough to get LSU past the second round of the NCAA tournament. For a third straight year, Shaq's quest for a national title had barely gotten off the ground.

After the tournament, Shaq decided he would not return to Baton Rouge for his senior year. He would make himself available for the NBA draft. It was not an easy decision. Shaq loved LSU, and he was getting good grades. Plus, his parents really wanted him to get a diploma. "The main factor was, if I went back to school the next year, would I have fun?" he says. "My dad told me when I was younger, if you're not having fun at what you're doing, it's time to do something else."

★ 5 ★

SHAQ ATTACK

The Orlando Magic had the second-worst record in the National Basketball Association during the 1991–92 season, winning just 21 games. The team owned the first pick in the draft, thanks to a lucky draw in the league's lottery, and they selected Shaquille O'Neal. Shaq was expected to transform a bumbling franchise into an instant success.

Shaq proudly displays his Orlando Magic jersey.

Shaq's quickness to the basket has made him unstoppable since his first NBA game.

To do this, he would have to prove himself a top NBA center from the opening tip-off. In his first game, Shaq tied the league record for rebounds in a pro debut with 18. A few days later, he became the first player ever to be named the NBA Player of the Week during his first week in the league.

As the season wore on, the Magic won their share of games and Shaq made his share of rookie mistakes. The real story, however, was how the big man energized pro basketball. The opponent's fans cheered as loudly for Shaq as the home fans did, and they bought millions of dollars worth of souvenirs featuring his name, number, and face. Some of his basketball cards were selling for hundreds of dollars, and it was impossible to turn on a television without seeing his boyish grin on one commercial or another.

Shaq easily beat out Alonzo Mourning for Rookie of the Year honors and was the only player to place in the top ten in scoring, shooting, rebounding, and blocked shots. And twice during his first season, he destroyed backboards with thunderous dunks, only adding to his fame. The only thing Shaq could not do was get Orlando into the playoffs. Although the team finished with a 41–41 record, it fell one win short.

Shaq's size became so legendary that he had a candy bar named after him—Mr. Big.

Shaq denies a pass into the middle. He has improved his defense each year.

★ ★ ★

But there was good news in the spring of 1993. Despite the overwhelming odds against it, the Magic earned the number-one pick in the NBA draft again. In a shrewd move, general manager Pat Williams selected Michigan's Chris Webber. Williams then traded Webber to the Golden State Warriors for the player he really wanted, Anfernee "Penny" Hardaway. Williams also got three first-round draft choices over the next seven years. With Shaq, Penny, Nick Anderson, and Dennis Scott, Orlando was on the verge of putting together a championship-caliber team.

Everything came together for the Magic during the 1994–95 season. Shaq developed several effective low-post moves, a little jump hook, and a turnaround jumper. Hardaway played brilliantly at point guard. And free-agent Horace Grant, the power forward on two NBA champion Bulls teams, provided leadership and muscle for the young Orlando squad. The team went 39–2 at home, won 57 games overall, and averaged a league-high 110.9 points per game.

***

The big story, of course, was Shaq. He not only led the NBA in field goals, points, and scoring average but proved he was every bit as good as his numbers in some memorable head-to-head match-ups. In one unforgettable week in March, Shaq took on the three top centers in the NBA: Patrick Ewing, Hakeem Olajuwon, and David Robinson. Shaq scored 41 points against Ewing, hauled down 20 rebounds against Olajuwon, and burned Robinson for 36 points and 12 rebounds.

The team faced its first big test in the second round of the playoffs against the Chicago Bulls. After splitting the first four games, the Magic won the pivotal fifth game and got a marvelous performance from their All-Star center. With the Orlando fans screaming louder than ever, Shaq shut down the lane and grabbed 22 rebounds in a 103-95 win. In Game 6, the Bulls seemed to have the game in hand when suddenly, Shaq, Penny, and Dennis Scott took over and scored the game's final 14 points to bounce a stunned Bulls

Shaq fights for position against the Philadelphia 76ers.

Shaq "clears the boards" against the Bulls.

33

team out of the playoffs. Next, the Magic
disposed of the Indiana Pacers in a tense,
seven-game series to win the Eastern Conference
championship.

Orlando's incredible run ended against the
Houston Rockets in the NBA Finals. Olajuwon,
who Shaq still claims is the best center in the
world, taught his young friend a major lesson
in what it takes to be a champion. Olajuwon
outplayed, outhustled, and outscored Shaq in
an embarrassing four-game sweep. A couple of
the games were close, but there was never any
doubt about which team was in control. Shaq
tried to learn from his mistakes and make
himself a better player. This would not be his
last trip to the finals, he vowed. The next time
the NBA championship was within reach, he
would be ready.

Shaq spent one more season in Orlando and
helped the team to a franchise-record 60 wins.
He finished third in the league in scoring and

A demoralized Shaq watches as the Rockets sweep Orlando in the finals.

shooting percentage, but the team was denied a return to the NBA Finals when they were swept by the Chicago Bulls. Due in part to a painful thumb injury, Shaq played poorly throughout the playoffs. Even more distressing was that, for the first time in Shaq's career, the fans in Orlando were questioning his effort. It looked as if he was letting himself get pushed around.

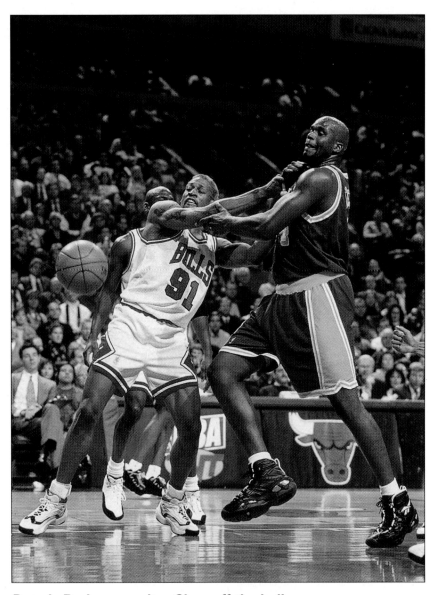

Dennis Rodman pushes Shaq off the ball.

What they did not realize is that Shaq is probably the "most-fouled" man in league history. During the playoffs, referees did not whistle opponents unless they really hacked him. "Guys like to lean on my arm, pin it to my side so I can't rebound," Shaq claims. "If you watch closely, you'll see it almost every play!"

After two straight near misses with the Magic, Shaq felt it was time to fulfill his longtime dream and play for the Los Angeles Lakers. He wanted to live in a place where he was not the only big star in town. He wanted to make his music, film his movies, and do his commercials in the center of the entertainment universe. And he wanted the mountains and the ocean and all of the other things Los Angeles had to offer.

Shaq's move to Los Angeles has enabled him to pursue his interests in film and music.

Shaq's arrival in L.A. has led to great expectations.

Coming to the Lakers meant that Shaq would be compared to the team's three great centers: George Mikan, Wilt Chamberlain, and Kareem Abdul-Jabbar. Each was the dominant center of his era, each brought a championship to the franchise, and each earned a place among the all-time greats. Was Shaq up to the task? This was, and still is, a subject of intense debate.

No one his size has ever moved with such grace and quickness. Shaq's feet are fast and his body control is superb. He is almost impossible to guard when he has the ball, and he is very hard to beat when he is on defense. But Shaq has one glaring weakness: He has never developed a consistent shooting touch. He can quickly ring up 40 points with short bank shots and slam dunks. But at the end of a close game, when free throws often determine the outcome, Shaq is just about the last guy you want on the line. Can a player be considered one of the all-time best if he cannot hit clutch free throws? Shaq has vowed to put

that question to rest. Perhaps he will answer his critics when an NBA title hangs in the balance.

Despite his tremendous ability on the floor, Shaq has never been able to make free throws with consistency.

Los Angeles Laker fans certainly hope so. They could not have been more pleased with the addition of Shaq. In the team's 1996–97 opener, he hit 10 of 12 shots in an easy win over the Suns. With Shaq among the league leaders in shooting, scoring, rebounding, and shot-blocking, the Lakers established themselves as the top

Shaq goes for a dunk.

Shaq rests an injury that sidelined him for 30 games in the 1996–97 season.

team in the Western Conference. But it was not just their new center who was producing; the entire team seemed to be coming together. If a key player went down, another stepped up to take his place. Guard Eddie Jones became a clutch three-point shooter and defensive player. Rookie Kobe Bryant developed faster than anyone had expected. Point guard Nick Van Exel matured as a floor general, and power forward Elden Campbell played extremely well at Shaq's side.

Sadly, what could have been a season for the ages turned into a disaster when, in a February game against the Minnesota Timberwolves, Shaq blew out his knee. The damage was bad: He tore a ligament, fractured a bone, and damaged the capsule surrounding the joint. The injury put Shaq out for 30 games and cost the Lakers the division title. The big guy came back in time for the playoffs, but he could not play at 100 percent, and Los Angeles lost to the Utah Jazz to end their season.

Is Shaq scared about proving himself in L.A.? Are you kidding? "Nothing scares me," he grins. "I'm an action guy. Scuba diving, bungee jumping, motorcycles—I'm there!"

The Shaquille O'Neal era has officially begun in Los Angeles. The eyes of the sports world are on Shaq, and the hopes and dreams of an entire city rest squarely upon his broad shoulders. Despite his off-the-court activities, he is all-business when he steps onto the hardwood. That is what Laker fans have come to expect and appreciate from their superstars, from Wilt to Kareem to Magic. Whether Shaq can deliver a championship remains to be seen. As we head toward the turn of the century, it undoubtedly will be one of the most fascinating stories in all of sports.

Los Angeles fans expect Shaq to improve his game and bring a championship back to their city.

C ★ H ★ R ★ O ★ N

1972	• March 6: Shaq is born in Newark, New Jersey.
1990	• Shaq enters Louisiana State University.
1991	• Shaq is named to the All-American first team.
1992	• Shaq leaves college and enters the NBA draft. The Orlando Magic drafts him with its number-one pick.
1993	• After his first season in the NBA, Shaq wins the Rookie of the Year award.
1995	• Shaq leads the Orlando Magic to the NBA finals, but they are swept by the Houston Rockets in four games.

O ★ L ★ O ★ G ★ Y

1996
- Shaq plays on the U.S. Olympic team that wins the gold medal in Atlanta.

- Shaq leads the Orlando Magic to a franchise-record 60 wins during the season, but they lose to the Chicago Bulls in the playoffs. Shaq decides not to return to Orlando and signs with the Los Angeles Lakers instead.

1997
- Shaq and the Lakers grab the lead in the Western Conference, but Shaq misses 30 games due to an injury. The Lakers make it to the Finals, but lose to the Utah Jazz.

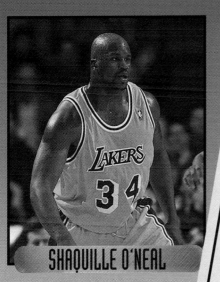

SHAQUILLE O'NEAL

SHAQUILLE O'NEAL

Born **March 6, 1972**

Place of Birth **Newark, New Jersey**

Height **7' 1"**

Weight **300 pounds**

Pro Teams **Orlando Magic, Los Angeles Lakers**

Awards **Two-Time All-American, 1991 College Player of the Year, 1993 NBA Rookie of the Year, 1995 NBA Scoring Leader**

NBA STATISTICS

Year	Team	Games	Rebounds per Game	Points per Game
1992–93	Magic	81	13.9	23.4
1993–94	Magic	81	13.2	29.3
1994–95	Magic	79	11.4	29.3*
1995–96	Magic	54	11.0	26.6
1996–97	Lakers	51	12.5	26.2
Total		346	12.5	27.0

* Led NBA

★ ★ ★

ABOUT THE AUTHOR

Mark Stewart grew up in New York City in the 1960s and 1970s—when the Mets, Jets, and Knicks all had championship teams. As a child, Mark read everything about sports he could lay his hands on. Today, he is one of the busiest sportswriters around. Since 1990, he has written close to 500 sports stories for kids, including profiles on more than 200 athletes, past and present. A graduate of Duke University, Mark served as senior editor of *Racquet,* a national tennis magazine, and was managing editor of *Super News*, a sporting goods industry newspaper. He is the author of every Grolier All-Pro Biography and eight titles in the Children's Press Sports Stars series.